Tough Topics

Bullying

Elizabeth Raum

Heinemann
LIBRARY

www.heinemann.co.uk/library
Visit our website to find out more information about Heinemann Library books.

To order:
☎ Phone 44 (0) 1865 888066
📄 Send a fax to 44 (0) 1865 314091
💻 Visit the Heinemann Bookshop at www.heinemann.co.uk/library to browse our catalogue and order online.

First published in Great Britain by Heinemann Library, Halley Court, Jordan Hill, Oxford OX2 8EJ, part of Harcourt Education.
Heinemann is a registered trademark of Harcourt Education Ltd.

Editorial: Rebecca Rissman and Diyan Leake
Design: Joanna Hinton-Malivoire
Picture research: Tracy Cummins and Heather Mauldin
Production: Duncan Gilbert

Origination: Dot Gradations Ltd
Printed and bound in China by South China Printing Co. Ltd

ISBN 978 0 431 90826 7
12 11 10 09 08
10 9 8 7 6 5 4 3 2 1

British Library Cataloguing in Publication Data
Raum, Elizabeth
Bullying
 302.3

A full catalogue record for this book is available from the British Library.

Acknowledgments
The author and publisher are grateful to the following for permission to reproduce copyright material: © Corbis pp. **7** (Michael Prince), **11** (Norbert Schaefer), **13** (zefa/Heide Benser), **16** (Kevin Dodge), **17** (Creasource), **18, 23** (Royalty Free), **20** (Little Blue Wolf Productions/Royalty Free), **25** (zefa/M. Thomsen), **28** (Najlah Feanny); © Getty Images pp. **6, 8, 9, 26, 29** (Royalty Free), **10** (Matt Henry Gunther), **12** (Catherine Ledner), **19** (David Roth), **21** (John Giustina), **24** (DreamPictures), **27** (Robert Burke); © Jupiter Images p. **4** (Corbis/Royalty Free); © Masterfile pp. **5** (Royalty Free), **15** (Raoul Minsart); © SuperStock p. **22** (BilderLounge).

Cover photograph reproduced with permission of © Jupiter Images/Corbis.

Every effort has been made to contact copyright holders of any material reproduced in this book. Any omissions will be rectified in subsequent printings if notice is given to the publisher.

The author would like to thank Ms Helen Scully, Guidance Counselor, Central Elementary School, Warren Township, New Jersey, USA for her valuable assistance.

Contents

Some words are shown in bold, **like this**. You can find out what they mean by looking in the glossary.

What is bullying?

Bullying is hurting, scaring, or leaving someone out on purpose. Bullying is unkind and unfair. Bullying hurts everyone.

▶No one wants to be bullied.

▼Bullying can cause hurt feelings.

Children may meet **bullies** at school or in their neighbourhoods. Many children are bullied. Other children worry when they see bullies hurting others. They may not know how to help.

▲Sometimes bullies form a gang.

Both boys and girls can be bullies. Bullies may hit, shove, or kick. They may call others names or make mean jokes about the way a child looks or acts.

Bullying also includes leaving someone out, **gossiping**, or being mean to another child. Bullies can act alone or in a group. Bullying hurts. No one wants to be laughed at or left out.

▲It hurts to be left out.

What if I'm bullied?

It's scary to be bullied. Remind yourself that you are a good person. You don't deserve to be treated badly. No one does.

▼Every person is special. No one should be bullied.

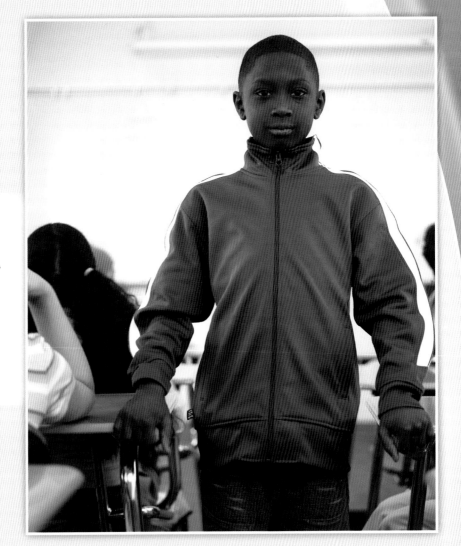

▶ Stand tall. It makes you look **confident**.

Bullies sometimes pick on children who are quiet and don't stand up for themselves. But anyone can be bullied.

▲ Try to smile when you face the bully. It helps you feel brave.

Act brave even if you are scared. Bullies want to make you cry. If you act as if the **teasing** doesn't bother you, the bully may give up.

Look directly at the bully. Then walk quickly toward an adult you trust. It's important to tell someone if you are being bullied.

▼ Look the bully in the eyes. This tells the bully that you are not afraid.

How to stay safe

Stay away from bullies. Join a group of children or stand by the teacher. If you are worried, tell a teacher.

▲Bullies are not likely to bother you if you are in a group.

Don't try to make a bully angry. Don't call the bully names or hit back. It just gives the bully a reason to **attack** you.

◄ Hitting back is a bad idea.

Tips for Dealing with Bullies

→ Be **confident**. Speak up for yourself.

→ Play in a group or near a teacher.

→ Shout if you need help.

→ Walk away. Don't fight back.

→ Tell a teacher or other helpful adult that you are being bullied.

Bullies might say things that make you feel bad. Tell yourself that the things the bully says about you aren't true. Say, "I like who I am."

◄ Shout loudly. Bullies don't want teachers to see what they are doing.

If a bully keeps bothering you, yell loudly. Shout, "Stop that!" or "Help!" and run to get a teacher or **playground supervisor**. Tell him or her what happened.

Make yourself bully-proof

It is very important to stay away from bullies. Stay with a group of friends. Bullies often pick on children who are alone.

▲You are safer with a group.

▲Friends make you feel stronger.

Find other children who look friendly. When you find children you think you can trust, smile. Say, "Hello." Join their games. Share your lunch. Be friendly to them, and they will be friendly to you.

◄ Make sure you feel safe on the way home.

If you walk to school, walk home with a friend. If you take a bus, sit near the driver. Sit beside someone you trust.

Stick up for yourself. Shout if something is wrong. Call out if you feel scared. Adults need to know if you are being bullied so that they can help you.

▼Always let people know if you need help.

What if I see bullying?

If you see someone being bullied, don't watch. Don't cheer. Shout, "Stop that!" or "Help!" Then run for help. Tell a teacher what is happening.

▲ Run for help.

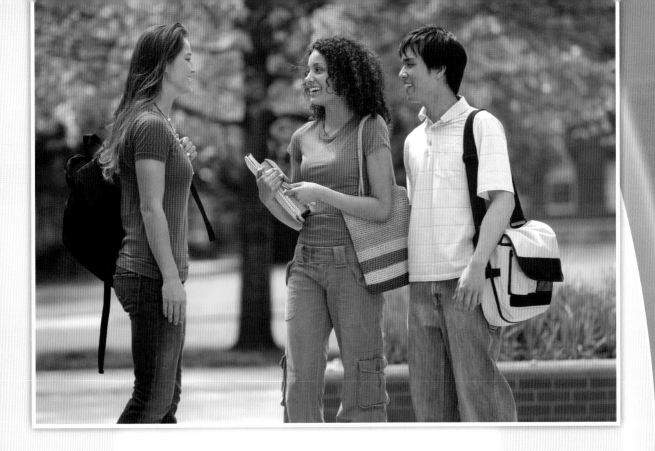

▲ Make room for others in
your group of friends.

When the danger is past, be kind to the
victim. Be sure to include him or her in
games. Bullies don't usually pick on
groups of people.

Am I a bully?

▲ Children don't want to spend time with someone who scares them.

Most children think that bullies are mean and unkind. They don't look up to bullies. Most children stay away from bullies.

▼ Many bullies get into trouble.

Bullies need help, too. Many bullies are sad and lonely. Bullies will feel better about themselves when they learn to be kind to others.

▲ Young children respect those who help them.

If you are a bully, practise being nice to others. Be kind to younger children. When others see you doing something good, they will begin to change how they think of you.

◄ Many bullies are smart. They can become class leaders.

Most bullies pick on others to feel better about themselves. There are better ways to make yourself feel good. Ask a parent or teacher for help.

Talk to an adult

Bullying is a big problem. School should be a safe place. Talk to your teacher or headteacher if you are worried about bullying at your school.

▲ These children feel safe at school.

▲ Teachers want to help.

Telling a teacher or headteacher about bullying is important. It helps keep you and other children safe. You are not telling to get the bully in trouble. You are telling to keep everyone from **harm**.

▲ This school does not allow bullying.

Most schools have rules against bullying. Ask your teacher or headteacher about these rules at your school. Every school should be a safe school.

▲School should be a safe place for everyone.

You can follow these rules to make school a safer, happier place for everyone.

- Do not bully other people.
- Try to help people who are bullied.
- Make sure that no one feels left out.

Glossary

attack fight

bully someone who hurts, scares, or leaves someone out on purpose

bullying when one person hurts, scares, or leaves someone out on purpose

confident sure of yourself

gossip unkind talk about other people

harm hurt

playground supervisor person who makes sure children are safe when they are in the school playground

prevention stopping something from happening

tease make fun of someone

victim someone who is hurt or harmed

Find out more

Books to read

Bullies, Big Mouths and So-called Friends, Jenny Alexander (Hodder Children's Books, 2006)

Don't Be a Bully, Billy! Phil Roxbee Cox (Usborne, 2008)

Good and Bad: Bully, Janine Amos (Cherrytree, 2006)

Thoughts and Feelings: Bullies and Gangs, Julie Johnson (Franklin Watts, 2007)

Websites

- ChildLine has a website (http://www.childline.org.uk/Bullying.asp) that gives information and advice on dealing with bullying.

- Kidscape (http://www.kidscape.org.uk/childrenteens/index.asp) is a group that works to stop bullying from happening.

- Bullying UK (http://www.bullying.co.uk/pupils/index.aspx) is a charity that gives online information and advice.

Index